63380

```
E
659.1     Greene, Carol
GRE       I can be a model
```

I CAN BE A
MODEL

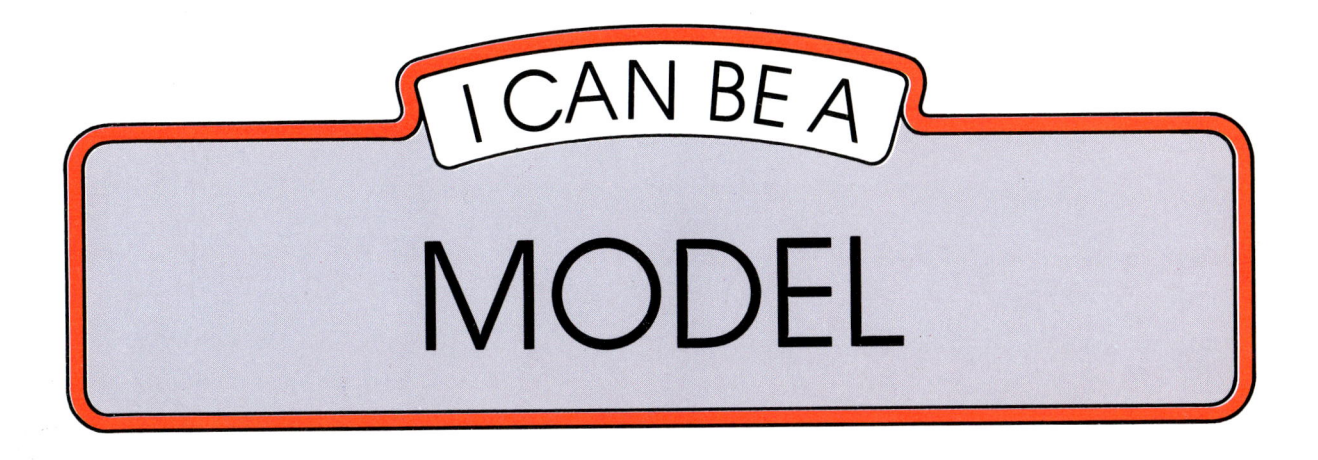

By Carol Greene

Prepared under the direction of Robert Hillerich, Ph.D.

CHILDRENS PRESS®
CHICAGO

Library of Congress Cataloging in Publication Data
Greene, Carol.
  I can be a model.

  Includes index.
  Summary: Discusses the requirements, condition, rewards, and other aspects of working as a model.
  1. Models, Fashion—Juvenile literature.
[1. Models, Fashion. 2. Occupations] I. Title.
HD8039.M77G74 1985   659.1'52   85-9676
ISBN 0-516-01887-6

Copyright © 1985 by Regensteiner Publishing Enterprises, Inc.
All rights reserved. Published simultaneously in Canada.
Printed in the United States of America.
  3 4 5 6 7 8 9 10 R 94 93 92 91 90 89 88 87 86

PICTURE DICTIONARY

booking

model   client

modeling agency

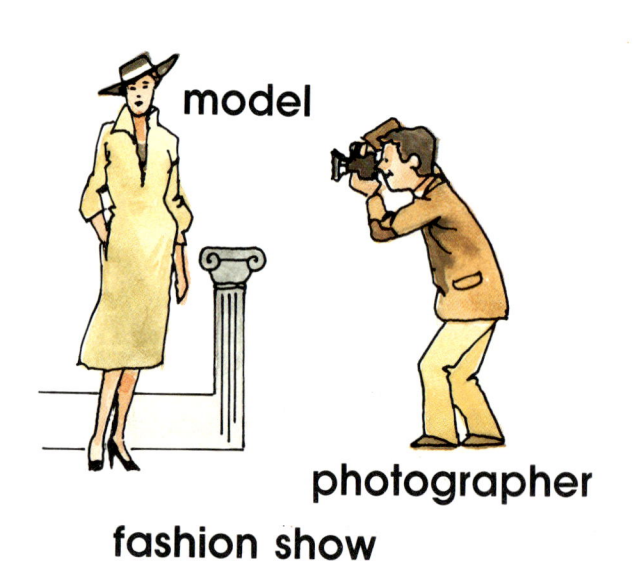

model

fashion show   photographer   companies

beauty contest

TV camera

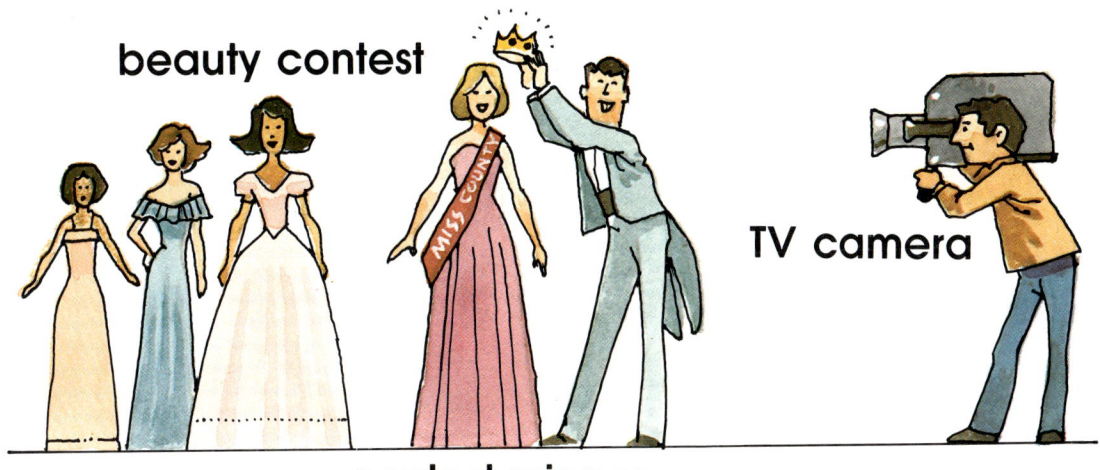

contest winner

ads

TV commercial

on location

fee

college

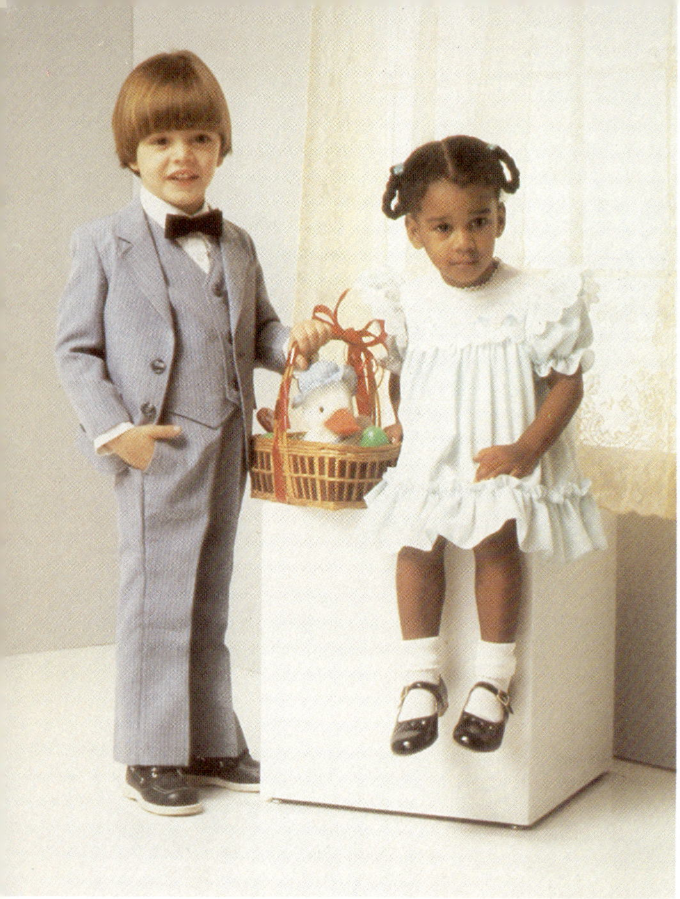
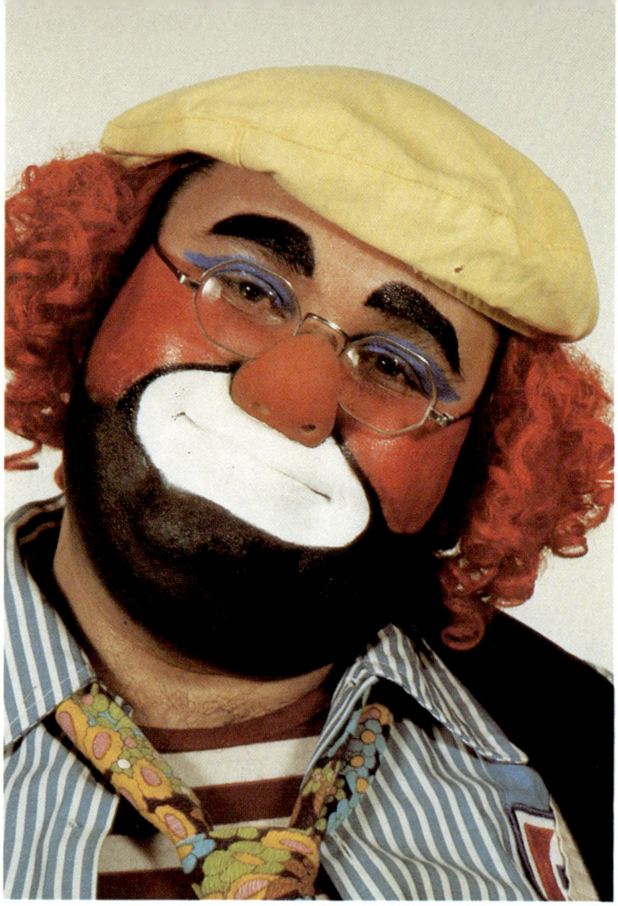
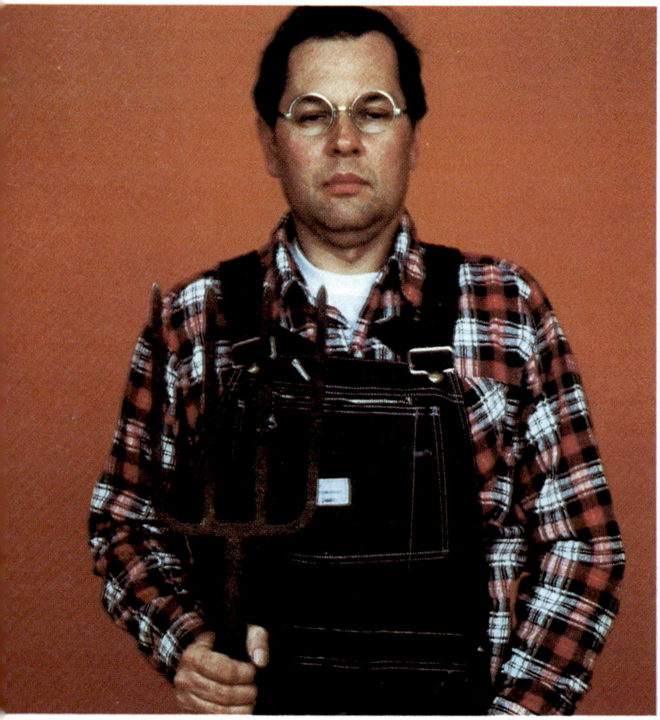
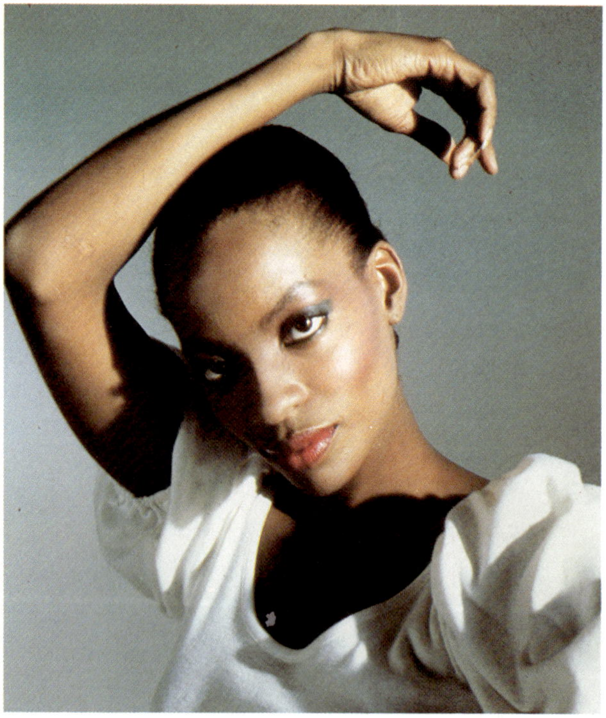

Only pretty girls can be models. Right? Wrong!

Models help sell many things. So there are many kinds of models.

Some are women. Some are men. Some are old and some are young. Children can be models, too.

model

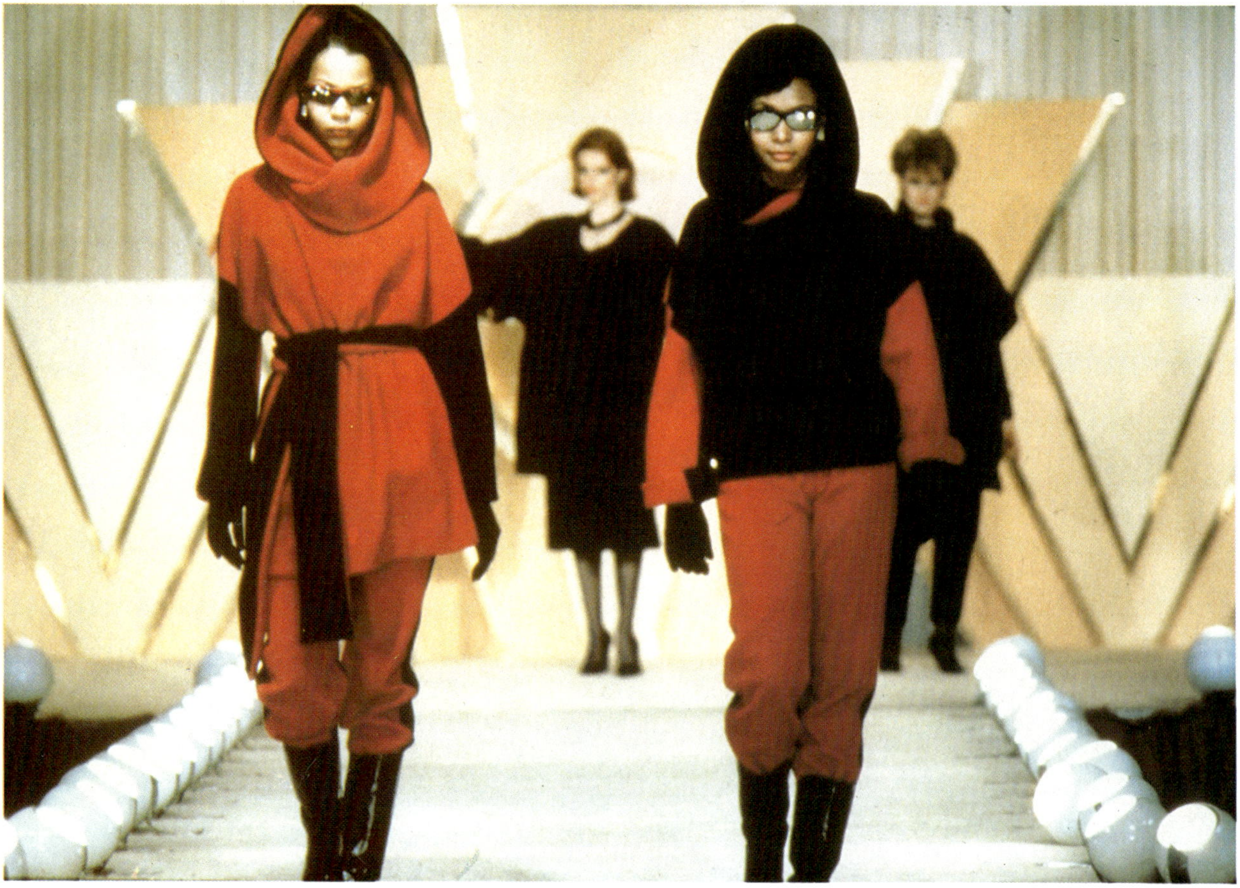

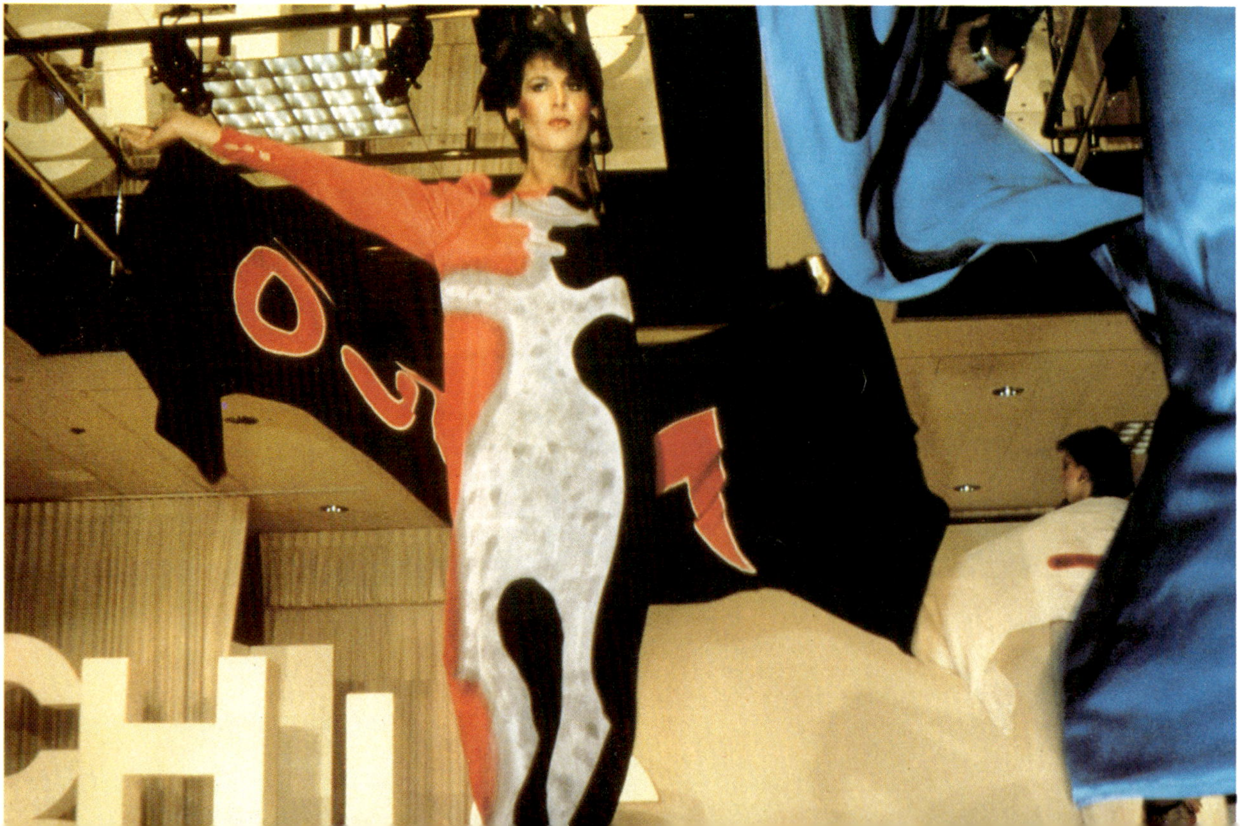

Fashion show models work hard. They must look so good that people will want to buy the clothes the models are wearing.

Some models work for companies that make clothes. Others work for stores that sell clothes.

These models wear the clothes in fashion shows.

companies

fashion show

7

Many people work behind the camera. Some put up the lights (above). Others build the sets (opposite page) that the photographer will use to take the picture.

8

Some models work with a photographer. The photographer takes pictures for ads. The ads go in magazines, newspapers, or catalogs. Some even go on billboards.

photographer

ads

Cameraman (on the ladder) shoots a video for a TV commercial

TV camera

TV commercial

Some models make TV commercials. They must speak and move around in front of a TV camera. Other people tell them what to say and do.

Camerman (above) shoots a commercial in a store.
Models (below) get used to seeing their ads on television.

Models cannot wear bathing suits in the snow. They cannot model ski clothes on a sunny beach. They must travel to a place that has the right weather for the clothes they are modeling.

This is called going on location. Many models like jobs on location.

on location

Models can be any size or age.

Models do not have to be beautiful or handsome. But they must be clean and healthy. They must stand up straight and stay in good shape. People must like to look at them.

Models must know how to act, too. Sometimes they have to look happy. Sometimes they have to look dreamy. Sometimes they get to look just plain silly.

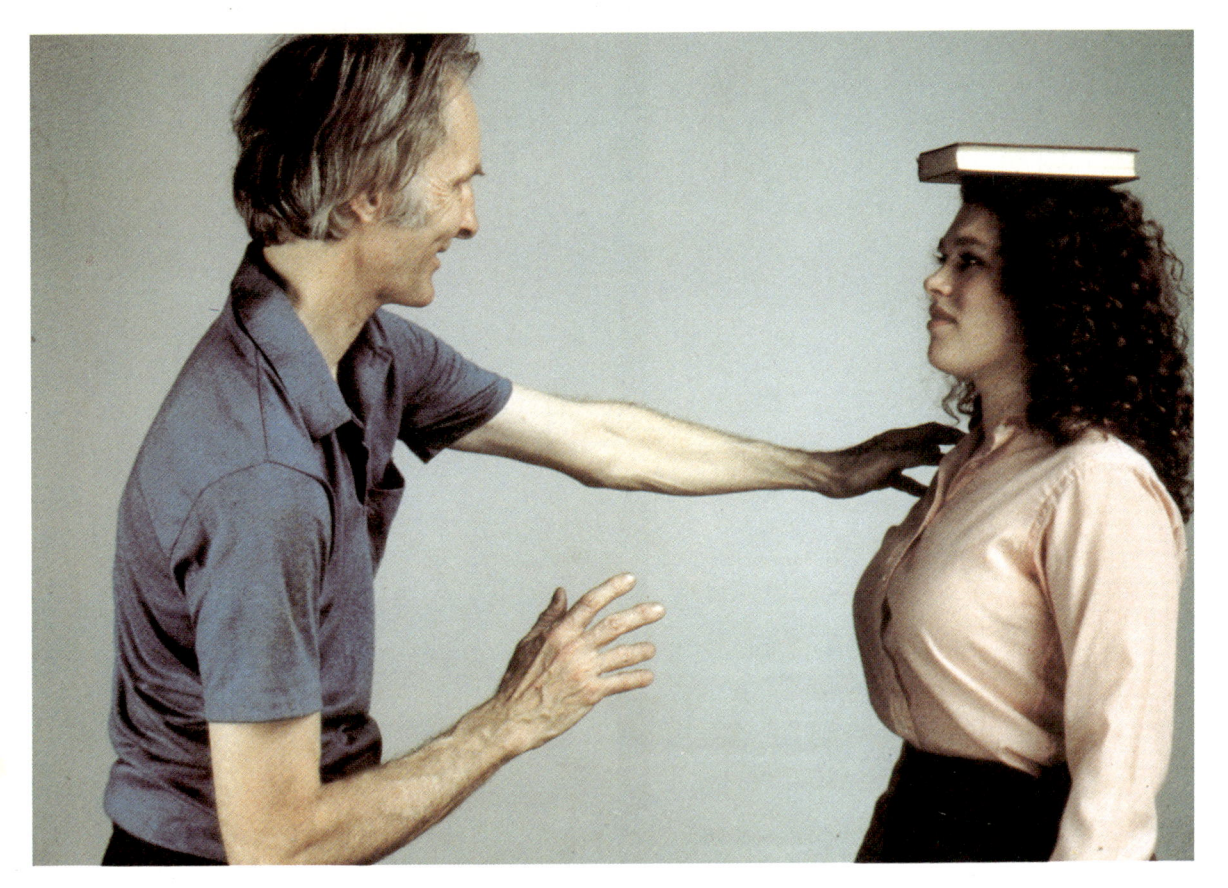

Models learn how to stand up straight and keep their head steady.

Beginners can learn how to model from classes. Or they can enter beauty contests. Contest winners sometimes get modeling jobs.

Agent discusses a modeling assignment with a client.

Some models get started by accident. A friend says, "I know someone who needs a model. Why don't you try out?" They do and—pow! They are on their way.

Many models work for agencies. The agencies help them get jobs. They make sure the models are treated well and get paid enough.

modeling agency

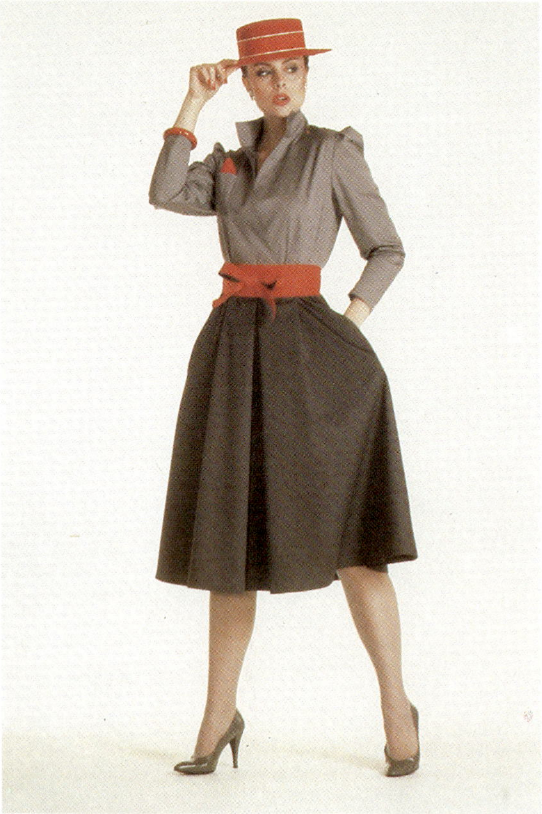
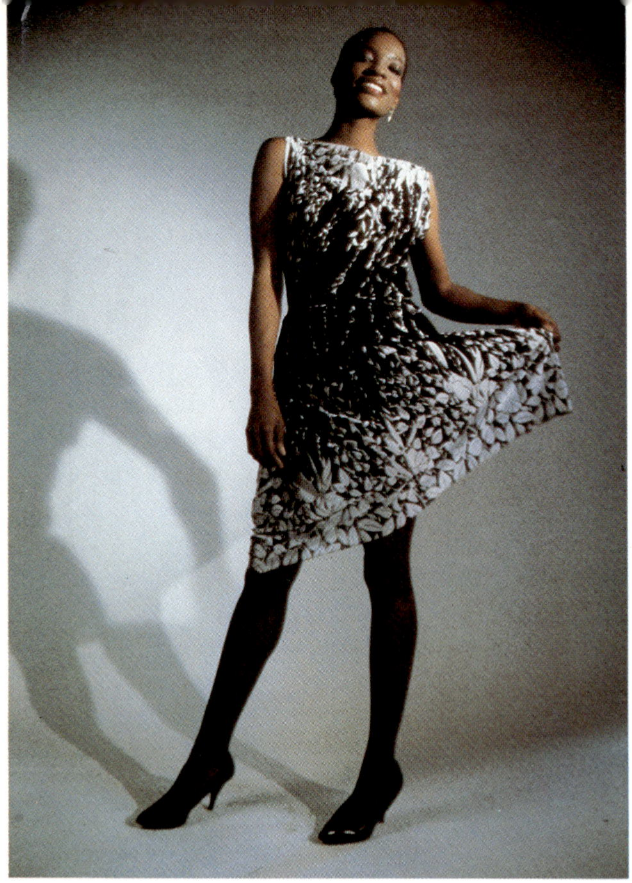
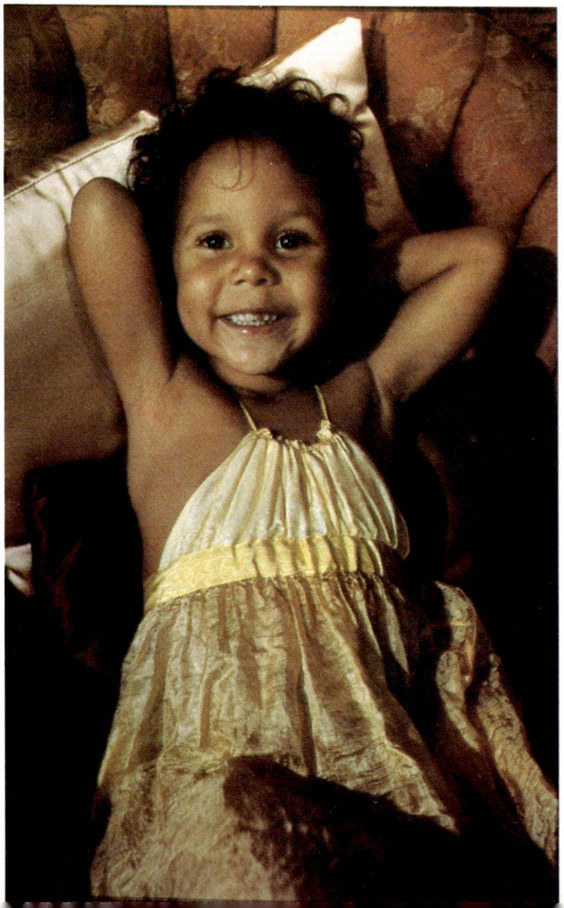
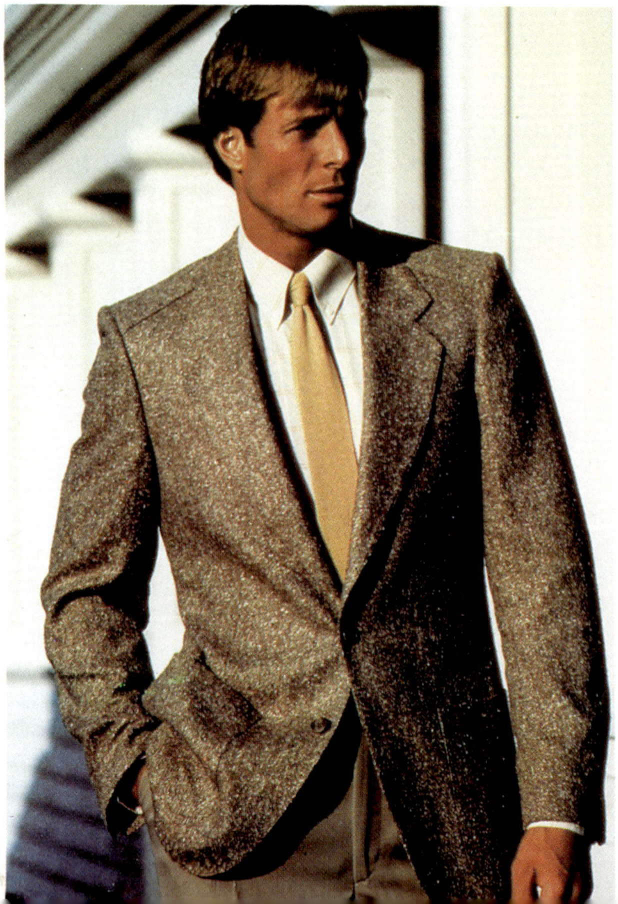

Agencies charge their models a fee. They also charge a fee to the people who hire the models. This is how agencies earn their money.

fee

People who hire models are called clients. Clients look at many pictures of models. Then they ask some of the models to visit them. These visits are called go-sees.

The model the client likes best gets the job. A model calls a job a booking.

A smiling model leaves a go-see.
Hurrah, she has a booking for the next day.

Sometimes models have many go-sees in one day. They may have several bookings in one week.

Models are hired to sell many different things (above). Many shots are taken (below left) before the right one is selected. For TV commercials the director (below right) must tell the model what to do.

Models use different makeup and hairstyles for different bookings. They must look just right for each job.

Models must work hard. It can take a long time to get one picture just right. It can take hours to make a short TV commercial.

Child models also work hard. But they must go to school, too. So they must work even harder.

Most models think their job is fun. They don't mind the hard work.

They like to see their pictures in magazines—especially on the covers. They like to watch themselves on TV. They like to hear people say, "You were terrific!"

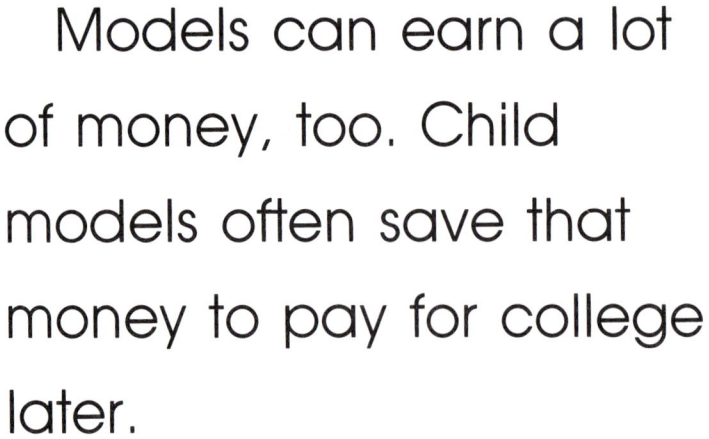

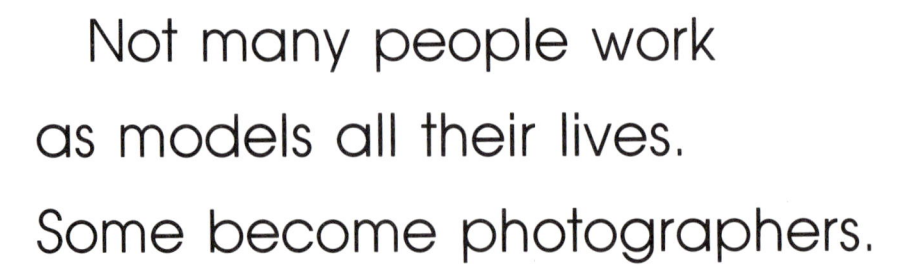

Models can earn a lot of money, too. Child models often save that money to pay for college later.

Not many people work as models all their lives. Some become photographers.

college

Some become actors or actresses. Some choose business or science or almost anything else.

But they never forget how it felt to be a model—great!

29

WORDS YOU SHOULD KNOW

ads (ADZ)--words and pictures that try to sell something

agency (A • jen • see)—a group of people who help other people get jobs

beauty contest (BYOO • tee KAHN • test)—a contest whose winners are chosen because of how they look and act

billboard (BILL • bord)—a large sign that advertises something

booking (BOOK • ing)—a job

catalog (KAT • ah • lawg)—a book of things for sale

classes (KLASS • ez)—places where people come together to learn

client (KLY • ent)—someone who pays someone else to do something

commercial (kuh • MURR • shul)—an ad on TV or radio

fashion shows (FASH • un SHOWZ)—gatherings where people see new clothes

fee (FEE)—a sum of money

go-see (go • SEE)—a visit by a model to a client

hire (HYRE)—to give someone a job for pay

model (MAHD • il)—someone who helps sell something by showing it

on location (lo • KAY • shun)—a place to which a model travels for a job

photographer (fo • TOG • rah • fer)—someone who takes pictures with a camera

TV camera (TEE VEE KAM • er • ah)—a camera that takes moving pictures for television

TV commercial (TEE VEE kuh • MERSH • il)—a short movie that tries to sell something

INDEX

acting, 16
ads, 9
agencies, 19, 21
beauty contests, 17
bookings, 22, 23
child models, 5, 26
classes, 17
clients, 22
clothes models, 7
fashion shows, 7
fee, 21
go-sees, 22, 23
kinds of models, 5
locaton, going on, 12, 13
magazines, 27
money, earnings, 28
photographers, 9, 28
TV commercials, 10, 25, 27

PHOTO CREDITS

Photos provided by Sears—4 (top left), 14 (bottom right), 20 (bottom right)

Image Finders:
 © Bob Skelly—4 (top right), 25 (right)
 © R. Flanagan—14 (top), 29

Hillstrom Stock Photo:
 © Art Brown—4 (bottom right), 15 (left), 17, 20 (top right and bottom left), 23, 25 (left)

Nawrocki Stock Photo:
 © Wm. S. Nawrocki—4 (bottom left), 15 (right), 26 (left)
 © Candee Productions—6 (2 photos), 7, 10, 11 (top), 16 (right), 24 (bottom right)
 © Carlos Vergara—9
 © Dirk Gallian—12
 © Jeff Apoian—13
 © Jim Whitmer—14 (bottom left), 26 (right)
 © Ken Sexton—18, 24 (bottom left)
 © Larry Brooks—24 (top)

Stock Imagery—8

ITT—11 (bottom)

Tom Stack & Associates:
 © Norman Mosallem—16 (left)

Candee Productions—20 (top left)

Spiegel—28

ABOUT THE AUTHOR

Carol Greene has a B.A. in English Literature from Park College, Parkville, Missouri and an M.A. in Musicology from Indiana University, Bloomington. She has worked with international exchange programs, taught music and writing, and edited children's books. Ms. Greene now works as a free-lance writer in St. Louis Missouri and has published around fifty books. Some of her other books for Childrens Press include *The Thirteen Days of Halloween, A Computer Went A-Courting, Marie Curie: Pioneer Physicist, Louisa May Alcott: Author, Nurse, Suffragette,* and *I Can Be a Football Player* and *I Can Be a Baseball Player* in this series.